folded Log Cabin Quilts

Create Depth in a Classic Block · From Traditional to Contemporary

SARAH KAUFMAN

C&T PUBLISHING

Text copyright © 2010 by Sarah Kaufman

Artwork copyright © 2010 by C&T Publishing, Inc.

Publisher: Amy Marson

Creative Director: Gailen Runge

Acquisitions Editor: Susanne Woods

Editor: Lynn Koolish

Technical Editors: Mary E. Flynn and Carolyn Aune

Copyeditor/Proofreader: Wordfirm Inc.

Cover/Book Designer: Kerry Graham

Production Coordinators: Jenny Leicester and Zinnia Heinzmann

Production Editor: Julia Cianci

Illustrator: Mary E. Flynn

Photography by Christina Carty-Francis and Diane Pedersen of C&T Publishing, Inc., unless otherwise noted

Published by C&T Publishing, Inc., P.O. Box 1456, Lafayette, CA 94549

Library of Congress Cataloging-in-Publication Data

Kaufman, Sarah.

Folded log cabin quilts : create depth in a classic block - from traditional to contemporary / Sarah Kaufman.

p. cm.

ISBN 978-1-57120-940-5 (soft cover)

1. Patchwork--Patterns. 2. Quilting--Patterns. 3. Log cabin quilts. I. Title.

TT835.K3828 2010

746.46'041--dc22

2009049460

Printed in China

10 9 8 7 6 5 4

Contents

Dedication

This book is dedicated to Judy Dafoe Hopkins, my dear friend since eighth grade in Juneau, Alaska. I was the new girl, introduced that first day of school and scared to death. Judy eagerly raised her hand and escorted me down to the cloakroom. We were friends within minutes! Some years later, back in Juneau for a class reunion, Judy and I were shown some patchwork squares a woman had made in a class. We were fascinated. Soon after, we both turned from garment making and needle-point to quilting. Now, we are approaching our "really significant" class reunion back in Juneau.

Judy has authored about twenty quilt books in the ensuing years. I, her greatest admirer, have enjoyed contributing quilts to her books whenever asked. What a thrill for me to translate my love of quilting and teaching this Folded Log Cabin technique into a book of my own! Now I can say, "Judy, I am an author too."

Acknowledgments

We were the Five Easy Piecers of West Linn, Oregon, in the early 1990s: Jane Calhoon, Joanne Perrin, Donna Smith, Sue Burgess, and me. We solved the problems of the world, while exchanging quilt books, ideas, and recipes. And we had great retreats! I owe the Piecers gratitude and much affection.

Along the way, a lovely book was passed around among the Piecers—*Great Little Quilts* by Eleanor Levie. A charming pleated Log Cabin quilt was one of the features, done in silks. Several of the basic measurements from this piece have been incorporated into my Folded Log Cabin blocks. Thank you, Eleanor Levie.

I am also grateful to Wendy Hill, quilt book author (her latest book is *Easy Bias-Covered Curves*) and friend, who offered helpful critiques as this book came together.

Thank you to Jean Wells Keenan, who gave me "go for it" encouragement. I've been privileged to teach Folded Log Cabin classes at her Stitchin' Post shop as well as at the annual Quilter's Affair in Sisters, Oregon.

And thank you to George Reay, friend, fisherman, and first-rate hunter of sticks. See George's discoveries in Hang It Up on page 20 and in the Gallery starting on page 45—many of the quilt hangers came from river-banks or the Oregon woods. We love picking up sticks with George.

Introduction

Early Days

My mother, Gudrun Pasma, was a couture seamstress. As a little girl, I loved her button box and the fabric scraps. With her encouragement, I made funny little doll blankets and scrappy houses that I hand stitched or glued onto a backing. I was a quilter, but I didn't know it yet. Years later, I made many quilts for my three children. Some of the quilts used the children's cherished old comforters as batting, which I "reupholstered" using pieced squares. I tied them on the only surface large enough to spread them out—the Ping-Pong table.

Following my marriage to Rich Kaufman in 1990, Shaw Island, in the San Juan mountains of Washington state, became our big adventure. We built a home with a fabulous quilt studio, I found quilt guilds, and I began taking classes. I loved intricate English paper piecing, appliqué, and Log Cabin quilts. Then, woe, I developed arthritis in my hands. Something had to change.

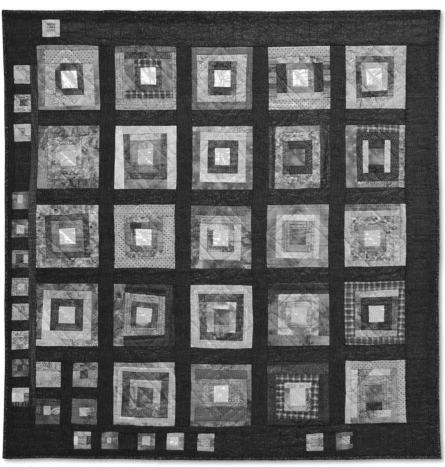

Log Cabin Glitz, 52″ × 54″, made by Sarah Kaufman, 2003

Log Cabin Glitz was my last regular, hand-quilted Log Cabin quilt. It hangs next to my bed, and I love waking up to this bright and cheerful piece. I will probably not make another Log Cabin quilt in this manner, and here's why: every strip needs to be pressed after stitching. In addition to the hand factor, constant ironing can easily distort narrow strips.

Snuggles, 60″ × 70″, made by Sarah Kaufman, 1992

I still love this quilt for its bold geometric wow factor. The soft and cozy quality makes it a favorite in our household. However, at 11½″, the blocks are too large, and there are strips of rayon mixed with cotton and wool, all cut from skirts and dresses from my businesswoman phase. Both the block size and fabric choices made construction a pressing nightmare.

Folded Log Cabin Quilts

I build these Folded Log Cabin blocks on a foundation, centering a 2″ square, and then layering 1½″ strips, which have been prepressed in half to ¾″ with the folds toward the center. These strips then stack in the same manner, resulting in tiny ¼″ logs. It is 90% machine sewing, with the iron now put away. Are you beginning to see the magic?

I am frequently asked, "Why don't you make bed quilts using this technique?" For starters, each block has five layers of fabric, plus backing—that's a lot of weight. In addition, the very density of these quilts makes them rather stiff. Extra stress on the very narrow seams is not recommended. A bed quilt needs to be able to handle plenty of use, and occasional abuse.

Think wall quilts—large or small—pillow tops, and table runners too. You will be thrilled to note that the density and weight of these pieces result in handsome, full-bodied art pieces. Batting is generally not needed in a Folded Log Cabin quilt.

Getting Started

A basic Folded Log Cabin block, sewn on a 7″ × 7″ muslin foundation, consists of 11 rounds of strips that have been pressed in half, stacked, and stitched around a 2″ center square.

Sewing Machines

Make sure your machine is always oiled and free of lint. You will be stitching through five layers of fabric, so a sharp needle is essential. It is nice, but not at all necessary, to have a state-of-the-art computerized machine. My Pfaff is sixteen years old. My mom's old Singer, circa 1954, does a fine job. Singer Featherweights can also handle the load; I see a few of them in every class I teach.

Traditional Log Cabin blocks in folds

Perfect Seams

The seams in these blocks are ⅜″ wide, so use a standard sewing foot, not the quilter's ¼″ foot. A walking foot can be helpful in keeping the block flat. If you pull on the seams as you stitch, the result can be a block that cups like a bowl. However, I have seen fabulous, perfectly flat work produced on a machine without a walking foot. It is all in the gentle care and feeding of each strip. I am very impressed with the built-in dual feed on my Pfaff, which works like a walking foot.

Thread

You will use a lot of thread, so be prepared. I recommend a neutral-color thread that either blends with your fabric choices or matches if there is a predominant color theme. For many of my quilt pieces I use tan or taupe. These tones, along with muted gray, blend in the best. In a perfect Folded Log Cabin quilt, the thread will never show, as it is covered up by the next folded log strip. Of course, perfect is rare (and that is probably a very good thing), so be conscious of your choice of thread color.

Lint buildup is reduced with a good-quality thread—my choices are usually Mettler silk-finish cotton and Superior Threads MasterPiece. Recently I have begun using Superior Threads' prewound bobbins, in the colors mentioned above—82 yards of long-staple Egyptian cotton thread in a bobbin is heavenly. (See Resources, page 48, for Mettler and Superior Threads.)

Fabric

I always look at fabric selection as the fun part of a quilt project. We are so blessed with fabulous cottons now. With budgeting in mind, if you use your stash, fat quarters, leftover scraps, and even leftover binding strips, and combine them with a special theme fabric, you'll generally find that everything works well together. A huge variety of fabric keeps me charged and happy. I so recommend feeling free to mix it up.

While I am a favored customer at our local quilt shops, I sometimes drop by thrift stores seeking fabulous garments to cut up. Oh, have I scored!

Bali, 11½″ × 18″, made by Sarah Kaufman, 2006

This quilt uses fabric from a Balinese-style batik dress.

All Zipped Up, 16½″ × 31″, made by Sarah Kaufman, 2008

Rarely can I make a quilt containing just two colors. I love the challenge of throwing in something odd or unusual to punch it up. For instance, I am very fond of black-and-white quilts but am nearly incapable of actually making one. The bold colors in the tiny center squares *of All Zipped Up* **make** this piece.

More Pizzazz

Embellishments and hanging devices are the other spices in my life. As you look through the book, note how often "just a quilt" can be transformed into a memorable art piece using embellishments and interesting methods of display. See pages 19–21 for tips on embellishing, hanging, and framing quilts.

Secrets of the Folded Log Cabin Block

The Formula

Yardages are based on 40"-wide fabric.

Here are some guidelines for figuring the amount of fabric you will need to make Folded Log Cabin blocks.

- A 7″ × 7″ block uses a total of approximately ⅓ yard of fabric.

- A 7″ × 7″ block uses approximately 6 strips, cut 1½″ × the width of the fabric to create all the logs in a block.

- 1 yard of fabric yields approximately 22 strips.

- For any of the 3 blocks shown on this page, ¼ yard of **each of 2 fabrics** is ample and will give you leftovers.

Note: The most carefully cut, folded, and stitched blocks will not always turn out to be the exact same size. Note the block back shown on page 13: there will be slight variations among your blocks as well. When your block sizes vary somewhat, refer to Measure, Modify, and Trim on page 16 for the best way to manage these "deviations."

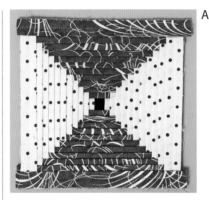
A

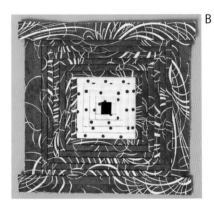
B

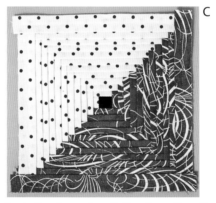
C

7″ × 7″ Log Cabin blocks: A. Courthouse Steps B. Courthouse Steps Squared C. Traditional

Cutting and Pressing Strips

For the best-pressed fold, rotary cut the strips 1½″ wide, crosswise from selvage to selvage. Yes, you can cut strips lengthwise along the selvage as well, especially if you want to feature a print or stripe going in this direction or to use up some binding strips. I often mist these lengthwise strips with water or light starch to aid in setting the crease. Use steam to press the strips in half. The ¾″-wide folded strips are ready for any Folded Log Cabin project.

If the fabric is thicker than normal cotton, or tends to ravel, I cut the strips about 1⅝″.

Mt. Bachelor in April

While at the ironing board, I enjoy the wonderful mountain view from my studio, watch TV, or listen to music. Pick your pleasure, and here's your reward: the bulk of your pressing is now done!

Start with a Foundation

For a basic Folded Log Cabin block (some projects in this book are different sizes), cut muslin foundation squares 7″ × 7″. With a pencil, lightly draw diagonal lines precisely from corner to corner. Center a 2″ square that contrasts nicely with your folded strips, matching each corner to the penciled lines. Ignore these lines after the center is in place.

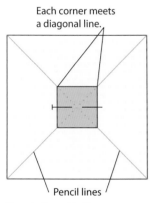

Each corner meets a diagonal line.

Pencil lines

Foundation with 2″ center square

I've learned from experience that blocks larger than 8″ × 8″ can get wonky, because it can be trickier to sew longer strips straight. It is okay to go smaller, though.

Sewing

I find it easier to position and sew strips for Folded Log Cabin blocks on the **left** side of the machine foot, with my work centered to the left as well. As you stitch, the **left** side of the foot should glide precisely **along the fold**. The stitching line **must be ⅜″ from the fold**. The **fold** is always your visual guide, not the raw edge. The width of a standard machine foot, or a walking foot, usually provides the ⅜″ rule. If you do not have a foot that provides the ⅜″, reposition the needle if your machine has this option.

Align your foot to the left of the strip, and stitch ⅜″ from the fold. Notice that the strip has not yet been trimmed to a log.

The Blocks

Each block style has a specific visual impact. I have no favorite—I love them all. And they all go together nicely in sampler-style quilts (see pages 30 and 43–47). In my Folded Log Cabin classes, I urge students to just choose one style and get started.

Courthouse Steps Block

Courthouse Steps block

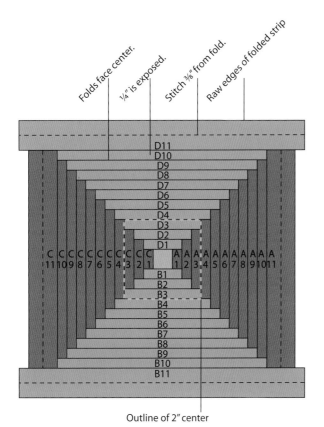

Folds face center.

¼" is exposed.

Stitch ⅜" from fold.

Raw edges of folded strip

Outline of 2" center

Courthouse Steps block

Making the Center

Start by centering a 2" square on a 7" × 7" foundation.

Making Round 1

1. From 1 pink folded strip and 1 blue folded strip, cut 2 logs, each 2" long.

2. Align the first pink log along one edge of the center square in the A1 position, with the fold to the center, matching up the raw edges of each strip to the raw edge of the center square. Stitch ⅜" **from the fold.**

3. Repeat Step 2 with the second pink log in the C1 position.

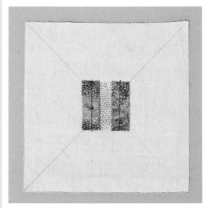

Starting Courthouse Steps (Note: Contrasting thread was used for visibility.)

4. Continue with the 2" blue logs in the B1 and D1 positions This creates the first round, and the center square is now a ½" pocket—take a second to make sure it is square.

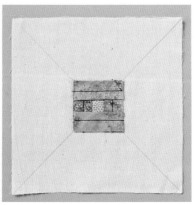

Courthouse Steps Round 1 complete (Note: Contrasting thread was used for visibility.)

Stacking the Logs

On with the block. Beginning at Round 2, put away your tools, except for sharp scissors. No more premeasuring to cut strips.

1. Starting again at side A, with an approximately ¼″-long flap* extending at the beginning, place a pink strip in the A2 position on top of the A1 log, **allowing ¼″ of width of the A1 log to show**. Stitch the Round 2 strip, again ⅜″ from the fold, starting where the A1 log begins and stopping where it ends.

2. Using scissors, cut the Round 2 strip at the other end, leaving another ¼″ flap on your new log. There is no need to sew down the flaps—just let them flap.

3. Add the next pink strip in the C2 position, allowing ¼″ of width of the C1 log to show. Then complete Round 2 in the same way at positions B2 and D2 with blue strips. Remember to leave a flap at the beginning of each strip as you place it, and again at the end when you trim the strip into a log.

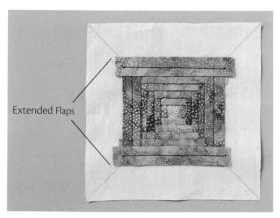

Courthouse Steps block, Rounds 2–5 (Note: Contrasting thread was used for visibility.)

*The flaps are critical for creating a stronger block. They provide cushioning for the next strip. **Do not skimp on this step**. My mistake piece, now a teaching tool, is a good lesson. I was short on fabric so I left off the ¼″ flap at each strip end, and you can see the result below.

Sarah's folly

Finishing the Block

1. To make a 7″ × 7″ block, aim for 11 rounds of logs.

2. Continue to check that the strips align with the muslin edges. If it helps to pin each strip, feel free to do so.

3. Consider the block finished when you have covered and gone just beyond the muslin foundation. When this is accomplished, those pesky muslin whiskers will be out of sight.

Back of block after 11 rounds

4. As you develop the technique, it is a good idea to occasionally check your work. Lift a log's raw edges to verify that you have encased the preceding log. A scant ⅛″ must show as a seam allowance.

Lift and check.

5. Refer to Measure, Modify, and Trim (page 16) to prepare blocks for finishing.

Courthouse Steps Squared Block

Squared block, Courthouse Steps variation (Note: Contrasting thread was used for visibility.)

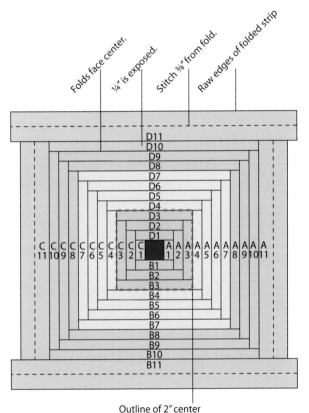

Folds face center.

¼" is exposed.

Stitch ⅜" from fold.

Raw edges of folded strip

Outline of 2" center

Courthouse Steps Squared block

Note: In the *Mix Master* project (page 30) and the Gallery (page 34), many of the blocks depict a squared effect with a variation in fabric placement. This is most effectively done with the Courthouse Steps technique, using the same fabric (or value) for all four sides of each round. Many of the early African-American Log Cabin quilts were made in this fashion. The term sometimes used for this style is "Housetop."

I frequently use this squared technique for the final few rounds to frame a traditional Courthouse Steps block. Have fun designing as you choose value and strip placement for Courthouse Steps Squared.

Traditional Log Cabin Block

Traditional Log Cabin block

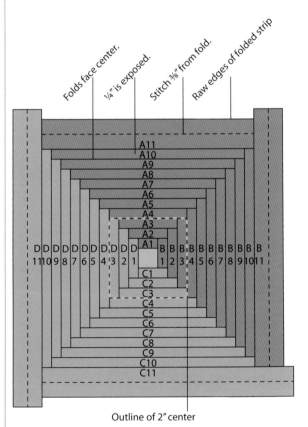

Folds face center.

¼" is exposed.

Stitch ⅜" from fold.

Raw edges of folded strip

Outline of 2" center

Traditional Log Cabin block

Making the Center

Start by centering a 2" square on a 7" × 7" foundation.

Making Round 1

1. From 1 pink folded strip and 1 blue folded strip, cut 2 logs each 2″ long.

2. Align the first pink log along one edge of the center square in the A1 position, with the fold to the center, matching up the raw edges of each strip to the raw edge of the square. Stitch ⅜″ **from the fold**.

3. Turn the block 90°, place the second pink log in the B1 position, and stitch.

4. Continue clockwise around the block, using the 2 blue logs in the C1 and D1 positions. Your value placement is now established. The center square is now a ½″ pocket—take a second to make sure it is square.

5. Starting again at side A, with an approximately ¼″-long flap* extending at the beginning, place a pink strip in the A2 position on top of the A1 log, allowing ¼″ of width of the A1 log to show. Stitch the Round 2 strip, again ⅜″ from the fold, starting where the A1 log begins and stopping where it ends.

Traditional Log Cabin block Round 1 (Note: Contrasting thread was used for visibility.)

Stacking the Logs

Beginning at Round 2, put away your tools, except for sharp scissors. No more premeasuring to cut strips.

*See Courthouse Steps block directions (page 13) for Sarah's flap rule.

1. Starting again at side A, with an approximately ¼″-long flap* extending at the beginning, place a pink strip in the A2 position on top of the A1 log, allowing ¼″ of width of the A1 log to show. Stitch the Round 2 strip, again ⅜″ from the fold, starting where the A1 log begins and stopping where it ends.

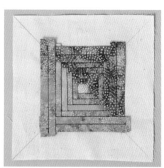

Traditional Log Cabin block, Rounds 2–5 (Note: Contrasting thread was used for visibility.)

2. Using scissors, cut the Round 2 strip at the other end, leaving another ¼″ flap on your new log. There is no need to sew down the flaps—just let them flap.

3. Add the next pink strip in the B2 position, allowing ¼″ of width of the B1 log to show, then complete Round 2 in the same way at positions C2 and D2 with blue strips. Remember to leave a flap at the beginning of each strip as you place it, and again at the end when you trim the strip into a log.

Finishing the Block

1. Feed each strip through gently, keeping it straight and aligned with the muslin edge as you position it in place and stitch.

2. Eleven rounds of logs will more than completely cover the 7″ × 7″ foundation. Remember to "lift and check" (page 13).

3. Refer to Measure, Modify, and Trim (page 16), to prepare blocks for finishing.

Using This Book

The project chapters will give you proficiency with these basic Log Cabin styles—done in folds. Try making some practice blocks first, adding a square of batting, then backing and binding—use them as potholders. I have made at least 100 of these little gems. Delighted recipients often say, "Gorgeous! I shall never use it!" These squares are also adorable framed (see *Rainy Sunday*, page 19). For me, a potholder or a memory piece often results from bits and pieces of strips remaining at the end of a project.

Potholder—leftovers from *East Meets Western* (page 29)

Courthouse Steps, finished with Courthouse Steps Squared

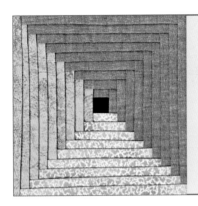

Joining, Sashing, and Finishing

After you have made the blocks, you need to put them together. Sewing the blocks with right sides facing together, as in regular block piecing, just doesn't work well. My technique is to zigzag the blocks together and then apply sashing strips.

Measure, Modify, and Trim

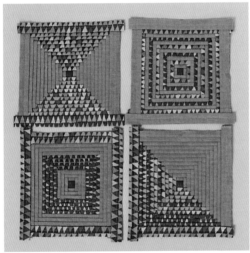

4 blocks to be joined; note that final flaps have not yet been trimmed.

First, the blocks must be sized the same. To begin, measure each block. For example, if 3 of 4 blocks are 7⅜″, these are deemed the perfect size. If the fourth block measures ½″ **smaller**, add a strip onto 1 or 2 sides. If the fourth block measures ½″ **larger**, you can remove 1 or 2 strips and either leave them off or stitch them back on very close to the previous round. The trick is to remake this block to match the others in size.

Yes, this modified block is a tad different from the others. But better this than attempting to ease it in or have it too small. The density of the blocks makes easing difficult.

Now it's time to trim off the flaps and give the blocks a final press. I like a shot of steam on both sides.

Joining the Blocks

Zigzag the raw edges of each block together, using the widest zigzag stitch on your machine. Butt the blocks together, and stitch to create rows. Then join each row in the same manner to complete the quilt piece. Happily, the blocks are hefty and will lie down nicely as you glide them through the machine.

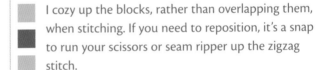

I cozy up the blocks, rather than overlapping them, when stitching. If you need to reposition, it's a snap to run your scissors or seam ripper up the zigzag stitch.

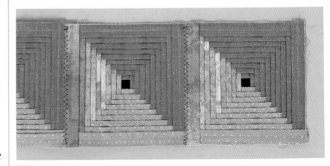

Zigzag blocks together.

Sashing

I tend to choose medium- to low-contrast fabric for sashing. If a high-contrast fabric is used, the grid that results can visually take over. *Sixty Cents* (page 35) features a no-contrast sashing.

The measurement for cutting the sashing strips is the same as for the block strips: 1½″ wide. You can also use leftover strips from the project, steam pressed open again.

1. Beginning with the first row (horizontal or vertical, your choice), place the sashing strip along the zigzag stitching and right sides together, with the raw edge of the sashing right next to the zigzag. Pin, making sure the sashing is visually straight.

2. Use a basting stitch on your machine to stitch this seam approximately ⅜″ from the raw edge. Remove your work from the machine, take out the pins, and examine. If you have essentially covered the stitching on the outer folded logs, congratulations. Go back and sew with a normal stitch length.

3. Lightly press the sashing strip over the zigzagged joint.

Vertical sashing over zigzag stitch

4. When all the strips are completed in one direction, turn under the unsewn side of the sashing, and hand blindstitch to the adjoining block. The sashing width should measure approximately ¾″.

5. Repeat Steps 1–4 for all the sashing in the other direction.

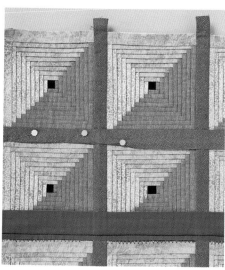

Horizontal row sashing

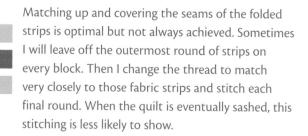

Matching up and covering the seams of the folded strips is optimal but not always achieved. Sometimes I will leave off the outermost round of strips on every block. Then I change the thread to match very closely to those fabric strips and stitch each final round. When the quilt is eventually sashed, this stitching is less likely to show.

Batting and Backing

Batting

Folded Log Cabin quilts don't require batting. They are weighty and hang beautifully, with plenty of body. However, if a border is added, this area does need batting, so that the density and loft equal that of the blocks. I save the ends and narrow strips of batting for just this purpose. After the borders are attached to the assembled blocks, cut batting strips 2″–3″ wider and longer than the border. Lift up each side, and loosely hand baste the batting to the folded log edges.

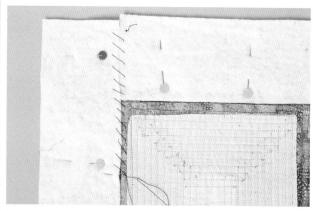

Attach batting.

Backing

Pin the quilt to the backing. You'll do a happy dance when you see how nicely it sets right down.

Quilting

The primary quilting needed on Folded Log Cabin quilts is on the sashing. I usually quilt with a tacking stitch called Crow Footing. I learned this stitch from Judy Hopkins many years ago, and I, who needed to depart from tiny stitches and tiny needles, became a happy hand quilter again. Judy offers these instructions in several of her quilt books and has kindly given me permission to explain my adapted version here.

#8 perle cotton thread is my choice for Crow Footing, together with a sharp tapestry or sashiko needle (see Resources, page 48, for Clover needles).

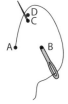 A lovely feature of folded logs is the ability to easily hide the beginning and end knots on top, beneath a fold.

1. Beginning at one end of a vertical sashing strip, bring your needle up at A. Loop the thread, hold it down with your thumb, and insert the needle at B, as shown. **Go through all the layers**, and bring the needle out at C. Insert the needle at D, which locks the stitch.

B-C: Go through all layers.

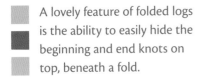

Crow Footing

2. Travel the needle **through the top layer only** to start the next stitch at A.

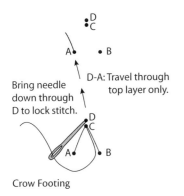

D-A: Travel through top layer only.

Bring needle down through D to lock stitch.

Crow Footing

3. Space the stitches 1″ or 1½″ apart. If it helps, draw a straight chalk line in the center of the sashing, and straddle this line with your Crow Footing stitch. Needle-nose pliers are useful to pull the needle out from a sashing intersection. We must be kind to our hands!

For the horizontal sashing, I like to make the stitches point in the same direction as the vertical lines of stitching. This means stitching them side by side. A little practice and it's easy.

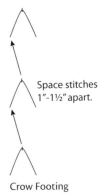

Space stitches 1″-1½″ apart.

Crow Footing

I try to blend or match the thread color to the sashing. For instance, if black thread were used on light-colored sashing, the thread traveling just under the top layer would be visible.

More Options

Feel free to experiment with other decorative stitches, by hand or by machine.

Embellishments are a fun alternative, and when stitched through to the backing, they do the same job as quilting. A stitch, bead, or button added to the center of the block is often a nice touch. The center pocket is perfect for inserting coins, washers, grommets—you name it.

For borders, the options for quilting by hand or by machine, and/or embellishing, are endless!

When the quilt is completed, pin it to your design wall. If the blocks pooch out in places, you can easily remedy this with a hidden stitch—**under a fold**, through to the backing, and knotted back on top, **under the fold again**. A simple fix, and it's our little secret!

Bind (single- or double-fold) your beautiful piece of art in your preferred method, but cut the strips 3″ wide for double-fold binding or 2″ wide for single-fold. A slightly wider binding—⅜″ to ½″—will encase the outside strip stitching line.

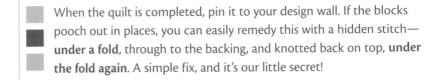

Things I Have Learned

Folded Log Cabin quilts are art pieces, that with reasonable care and attention should, have a long life. One of my earlier pride-and-joy quilts, transported from Hawaii in a container ship, was unfortunately folded in a packing crate for four weeks. It is permanently creased. No amount of pressing can rectify this sad outcome. Lesson learned: Now **all** my Folded Log Cabin quilt pieces are either hung or stored rolled on tubes. Whether you are storing or transporting, **do not fold** your Folded Log Cabin quilt. Fabric shops often have heavy cardboard tubes they are happy to give away. Pool swim noodles work well and can be cut to shorter lengths with scissors. Sheeting, batting, or acid-free paper should be wrapped around either a noodle or a tube before rolling the quilt on it.

Hanging, Framing, and Embellishing

Frame It Up

My first rule of thumb: **Begin with the frame**, then design the quilt piece to fit. I love scouring antique shops and thrift stores for old frames. Retail stores often have perfectly awful art in very nice frames, and priced to sell. The alternatives to the "begin with the frame" rule are to have your masterpiece framed by a professional or to assemble your own frame.

Whether you do your own framing or hire a pro, the following are some tips:

- In general, I don't use glass with framed pieces. Textiles need to breathe. I am more concerned with displaying a quilt away from bright sunlight than with a speck of dust or a bug daring to land on my precious quilt.

- If you do choose to frame using glass, spacers between the fabric and glass are important—it's the breathing again. A professional framer will know this trick, and I have purchased these spacer bars from a frame shop.

With *Rainy Sunday* (below), first came the frame that I found in a thrift store. After I made the blocks (sized ½″ larger than the frame openings), I attached a binding to each but left the outer edges of the binding unfinished. I cut a piece of fast2fuse stiff interfacing (see Resources, page 48) 1″ smaller than the frame back. With penciled lines on one side of the fast2fuse as a guide, I pressed the blocks onto each marked square. I positioned the quilt onto the back of the frame and stapled down the outside edge of the fast2fuse. Done!

The larger frames in my collection are newly constructed from old timbers—they just look old. It's easy to re-create these frames with simple tools and some paint-rubbing skills. Old window frames can be transformed into quilt frames too.

Each framed piece shown here and on the next page was an experiment in attaching the quilt to the frame. I am most pleased with the method of leather strips sewn down by hand in both directions on the back of the quilt. The strips are then threaded through small screw eyes inserted in the frame at intervals. The leather can be stapled to the back of the frame or doubled back and restitched to the quilt backing. Craft and bead stores are my source for leather, sold by the foot or by the spool. Narrow grosgrain ribbon also works well in this method.

Rainy Sunday, 25″ × 11½″, made by Sarah Kaufman, 2009

Smith Rock, 16½″ × 25″, made and framed by Sarah Kaufman, 2006

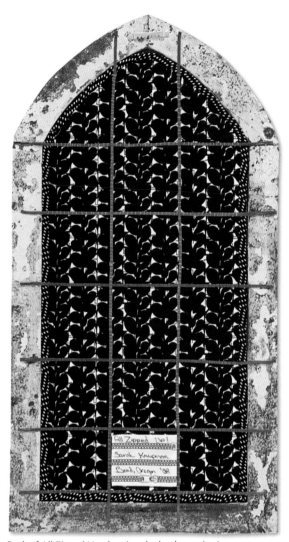

Back of *All Zipped Up*, showing the leather stripping connectors (front of quilt on page 9)

Hang It Up

While residing in Hawaii, my quilts took on a tropical, Asian look. I often displayed them on bamboo poles, Indonesian tapestry rods, and Japanese hangers.

Balinese Prada, 66″ × 46″, made by Sarah Kaufman, 2001

The quilt is suspended from a wood hanger from Indonesia. This type of hanger is commonly used to display tapestries.

After our move to central Oregon (high-desert country), my quilts, as well as my hangers, started to reflect this region and our casual lifestyle. In addition to galled sticks, I seek out rustic farm implements in local antique stores. My favorites are **singletrees**, which were once used to connect horse or oxen yokes. They can be found in antique shops and online (Google "singletree").

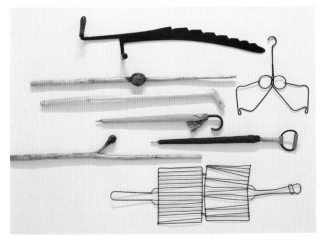

Sticks and rustic hangers

My latest acquisition (shown in the photo above) is the old wood-handled umbrella. It is next in line for a Folded Log Cabin quilt and will be adorned with a hanging doodad.

99% Marimekko, 20½″ × 18″, made by Sarah Kaufman, 2008

This quilt is hung using a singletree.

More Hanging Ideas

Loops stitched into the top binding are simple and do the job. See *Copper and Pewter, Mixed with Concrete* (page 29).

Most of my pieces attached to a hanging device have a sleeve that is attached in the conventional manner. A wood slat, with holes drilled at each end, is inserted into the sleeve. Leather strips or cording inserted into the holes can be tied to the hanger. Sometimes I slip 2″ (or larger) rings onto each end of a sturdy pole (instead of a slat) and then attach the rings to the decorative hanging device. Rings can be found in craft stores in the purse- and bag-making department. Wood curtain rings are also perfect for this use.

 Single-prong metal robe hooks from the hardware store work very well for easily displaying a hanging device. They come in a variety of finishes.

Even More Ideas

Future hang-ups

My future hang-up collection consists of (new and old) hooks, bells, spurs, spindles, Christmas tree ornaments, purses, and other curiosities. They will all be making a statement, dangling from a quilt hanger—someday. Seeking out these assorted trinkets is a favorite pastime of mine, besides shopping for fabric, of course.

Silver Threads Among the Gold

Finished block size: 7″ × 7″   **Finished quilt size:** 29″ × 29″

Silver Threads Among the Gold, made by Sarah Kaufman, 2009

I added some silver and gold threads to this quilt, in the form of glitzy folded strips, mixed in with the gray hand-dyed fabric. I couldn't help myself! As a result, the quilt got its name even before I found the gold slotted conchos that became the embellishment.

If you are wondering what conchos are and where you can find them, they often adorn Western wear. Ribbon streamers can be inserted into the slots. I found the gold heart conchos in a bargain basket at a leather goods manufacturing business. (Sorry, I bought them all.) I have Googled "slotted conchos" and found many different styles.

MATERIALS

- Gray solid fabric: 1½ yards for blocks and sashing
- Print fabric: 1½ yards for blocks and sashing
- Center square fabric: 1 strip 2″ × 20″
- Border fabric: ¾ yard
- Binding fabric: ⅓ yard
- Backing fabric: 1 yard
- Muslin for foundations: ⅝ yard
- Batting for borders: 2 strips 7″ × 22″; 2 strips 7″ × 32″

CUTTING

Refer to pages 10–11 for strip cutting and pressing.

From gray solid fabric: Cut 28 strips 1½″ wide.

From print fabric: Cut 29 strips 1½″ wide.

From center square fabric: Cut 9 squares 2″ × 2″.

From silver and gold fabric: Cut 2 strips each 1½″ wide.

From muslin: Cut 9 squares 7″ × 7″ for foundations.

From border fabric: Cut 4 strips 5″ wide.

From binding fabric: Cut 4 strips 3″ wide for double-fold or 2″ wide for single-fold binding.

Directions

MAKE THE BLOCKS

Refer to pages 12–13 for Courthouse Steps block construction.

Note: If you begin with gray solid fabric at A and C, you will always end up with print fabric at B and D—the final (widest) outside strips.

1. Center a 2″ center square on a marked foundation.

2. Cut 2 strips 2″ long from the print fabric and 2 strips 2″ long from the gray solid fabric.

3. Place the first gray solid 2″ strip on the center square at A, with the fold toward the center, matching up the raw edges. Stitch ⅜″ **from the fold**. Repeat with the other gray solid strip at C (opposite).

4. Continue with 2 print 2″ strips at B and D. Make sure that the center pocket is square.

5. Round 2 to Round 11 follow in the same order. Always begin at A. Remember to leave a **flap** at each end of every strip (page 13)—it's Sarah's sturdy block rule! You can randomly add shiny silver and gold strips in among the gray strips as you progress through the rounds.

6. After 11 rounds, the strips should cover the muslin foundation.

As you stitch the Courthouse Steps blocks, don't cut the threads for the first 4 or 5 rounds. Instead, gently turn the block around from A to C, stitch, and continue turning. When the blocks are completed, flip them over and snip the bobbin threads on the back.

ASSEMBLY, SASHING, AND FINISHING

Refer to pages 16–18 for block assembly, sashing, and finishing.

1. Square up the blocks, and determine their placement on a design wall.

2. When you are satisfied with your block arrangement on the design wall, zigzag stitch the blocks together, using the widest zigzag stitch on your machine. Refer to Joining the Blocks (page 16).

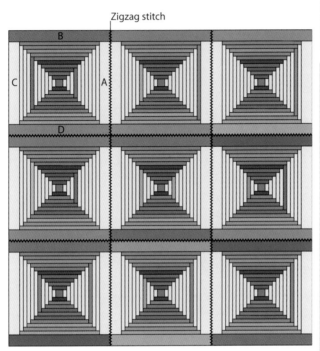

Blocks ready for sashing

3. Sash over the zigzag stitch, beginning with the gray vertical strips. Then, attach the horizontal print sashing strips. Refer to Sashing (pages 16–17).

4. Next add the border strips, and attach strips of batting beneath the border (refer to page 17 for adding batting to the border).

5. Place the quilt top on the backing, and pin everything in place.

6. Quilt the sashing and border in your preferred method. I used a Crow Footing stitch (pages 17–18) on both the sashing and border. The gold slotted conchos were added last. Beading would be a lovely alternative.

7. Bind the quilt with single- or double-fold binding.

GALLERY OF COURTHOUSE STEPS BLOCKS AND QUILTS

I love the symmetry of Courthouse Steps Log Cabin blocks. The steps can be the predominant design or disappear completely. The following blocks and quilts show a host of variations. Note how well Courthouse Steps and Courthouse Steps Squared blocks combine with Traditional Log Cabin blocks in the Gallery on pages 43–47.

7″ × 7″ finished block: The subtle mix-up of many blue fabrics is a fun twist. Sometimes it takes several rounds before the Courthouse Steps pattern emerges.

7″ × 7″ block from *Spindle and Blocks* (page 46): The centers in this 6-block piece began with 2½″ squares. Ten rounds complete the blocks.

Log Cabin Christmas, 24″ × 24″, made by Hiroko I. Ono, 2002

Hiro has an enviable fabric collection. For this quilt, she used only a few strong-value prints, which accentuated the Courthouse Steps.

Cow Bell, 20″ × 23″, made and framed by Sarah Kaufman, 2008

The bell reads "Wakefield Dairy, 1923." The funky wood frame was easy to match with my earthy fabrics and old wooden beads.

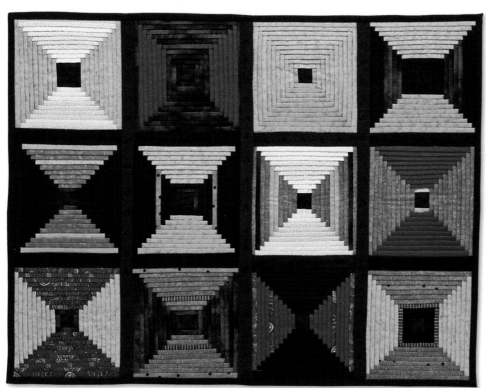

Zoom Lens, 29″ × 22½″, made by Sarah Kaufman, 1998

Photographers love this quilt. I noticed the zoom lens effect after the quilt was finished. The centers are 2½″ squares. Matching the black fabric for the first and/or second round makes a few centers appear larger.

B Is for Blue Blocks

Finished block size: 7″ × 7″   **Finished quilt size:** 28″ × 42″

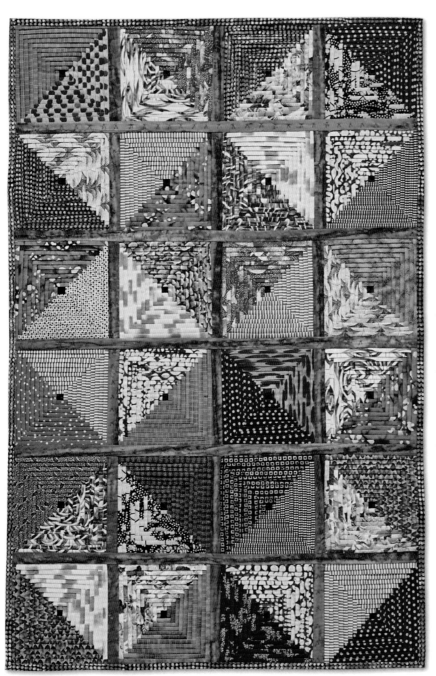

B Is for Blue Blocks, made by Sarah Kaufman, 2005

This is truly a scrap quilt. Of course it can be done with just two blues, but what would be the point? The fun for me is in using up some fabrics from my stash and playing with value. There is one medium-value fabric used for both light and dark. (Can you find it?) The simple rule for this quilt is to place medium-value fabrics next to fabrics that are either lighter or darker so there is good contrast. As you select possible fabrics, use a design wall, and take some time to play. A digital camera, a reducing glass, and someone else's eye are all helpful in achieving the final perfect image.

B Is for Blue Blocks, *in Traditional Log Cabin block style, is arranged in a pattern called Checkerboard, or Light and Dark. And please, if blue is not your hot color, use a color that is.*

MATERIALS

Approximately 6–7 yards of blue fabrics were used for 24 blocks: 40% lights, 40% darks, and the remaining 20% medium values. Most fabrics were used twice, and a ¼-yard scrap of dark blue fabric got into the mix and was used once. Try flipping some prints to the back side—sometimes the reverse side works nicely for a lighter value.

- Light blue fabrics: 2½ yards total
- Dark blue fabrics: 2½ yards total
- Medium blue fabrics: 1¼ yards total
- Center square fabric: ¼ yard that contrasts with block fabrics
- Sashing fabric: ½ yard
- Binding fabric: ½ yard
- Backing fabric: 1⅓ yards
- Muslin for foundations: 1⅛ yards

 If your blocks appear busy, select sashing fabric with greater contrast. This will help contain and calm them.

CUTTING

Refer to pages 10–11 for strip cutting and pressing.

From light-value fabrics:
Cut 58 strips 1½″ wide.

From dark-value fabrics:
Cut 58 strips 1½″ wide.

From medium-value fabrics:
Cut 28 strips 1½″ wide.

From center square fabric:
Cut 24 squares 2″ × 2″.

From sashing fabric:
Cut 8 strips 1½″ wide.

From binding fabric: Cut 4 strips 3″ wide for double-fold or 2″ wide for single-fold binding.

From muslin: Cut 24 squares 7″ × 7″ for foundations.

Directions

MAKE THE BLOCKS

Refer to pages 14–15 for Traditional Log Cabin block construction.

1. Center a 2″ center square on a marked foundation.

2. Cut 2 strips 2″ long from light fabric and 2 strips 2″ long from dark fabric.

3. Place the first light 2″ strip on the center square at A, with the fold toward the center. Stitch ⅜″ **from the fold**. Repeat with the second light 2″ strip at B.

4. Continuing clockwise around the center square, repeat with 2 dark 2″ strips at C and D. Your value placement is now established.

5. Continue with Round 2, beginning at A. Exposing ¼″ of the Round 1 strip, position this light strip, and stitch, again at ⅜″ from the fold. Remember to leave a **flap** at each end of every strip (page 13)—its Sarah's sturdy block rule!

6. Continue the block for 9 more rounds of strips, for a total of 11 rounds. Your strips should cover the muslin foundation.

As you make each block, enjoy the process of mixing up the values, trying some contrast tricks with medium-value fabrics.

ASSEMBLY, SASHING, AND FINISHING

Refer to pages 16–18 for block assembly, sashing, and finishing.

1. Square up the blocks, and determine their placement on a design wall.

2. When you are satisfied with your block arrangement on the design wall, zigzag stitch the blocks together, using the widest zigzag stitch on your machine.

3. Sash over the zigzag stitch.

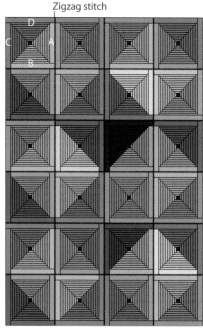

24 blocks, Light and Dark, or Checkerboard, pattern

4. Place the quilt on the backing, and pin everything in place.

5. Quilt the sashing in your preferred method.

6. Bind the quilt with single- or double-fold binding. The binding should be approximately ⅜″ to ½″ wide, to cover the outside edge of the blocks.

More Pattern Options

There was no end in sight with regard to my vast blue fabric collection, and, as always, there were leftover strips. So I continued on, making blue blocks with more classic Traditional Log Cabin design options in mind. Here are two more options for arranging the blocks. Note the medium-value fabrics used as both light and dark.

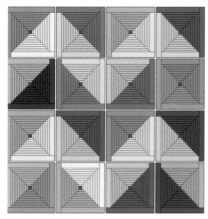

16-block Streak of Lightning

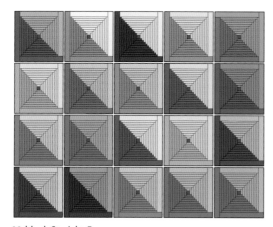

20-block Straight Furrows

But wait. By using **all** of the Streak of Lightning and Straight Furrows blocks (a total of 36), I could make a Barn Raising. Sixteen blocks complete the inner square (shown at right). For still more drama, one more complete round (an additional 20 blocks) is an even bigger scene stealer.

Inner boundary encloses 16 blocks (30″ x 30″ quilt)

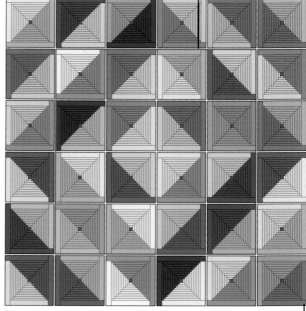

Additional 20 blocks (45″ x 45″ quilt)

Barn Raising, or Sunshine and Shadows

GALLERY OF TRADITIONAL LOG CABIN QUILTS

Traditional Log Cabin quilts made in Folded Log Cabin style can have the look of century-old quilts or appear as contemporary as you like.

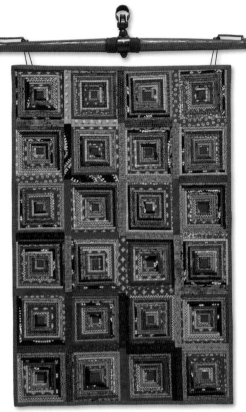

East Meets Western, 28½" × 43", made by Sarah Kaufman, 2007

A combination of Asian indigos, some hand-dyes, and my vast red collection all worked together with the old Western painted buggy connector hanger.

Copper and Pewter, Mixed with Concrete, 30" × 27", made by Sarah Kaufman, 2004

From the collection of Janet and Gary Gehlert. Suspended from handcrafted Alaskan willow cane.

Logs and Labels, 32" × 46", made by Sarah Kaufman, 2005

I collect clothing labels like some people save stamps! They are perfect for tucking into Folded Log Cabin strips.

Ab-Original, 25" × 32", made by Sarah Kaufman, 2006

An exhibit of Aboriginal tapestries at the Seattle Art Museum inspired this quilt. Rectangular blocks are a nice change.

Mix Master

Finished block size: 7″ × 7″   **Finished quilt size:** 14″ × 42″

Mix Master, made by Sarah Kaufman, 2009

Mix Master is a Folded Log Cabin block sampler—ideal for a table runner or a statement-making wall quilt. Study this piece and you will quickly identify two Traditional Log Cabin blocks; the rest of the blocks are Courthouse Steps and Courthouse Steps Squared.

An easy rearrangement of the blocks is three blocks by four blocks—a dramatic alternative. Sometimes I arrange, rearrange, and leave blocks on the design wall for a day or more. Eventually the piece tells you when it's right.

MATERIALS

- 2 dark red print fabrics: 1 yard total

- 2 medium red print fabrics: ⅝ yard total

- 2 muted gold print fabrics: ¾ yard total

- 3 not-quite-black print fabrics: 1 yard total

- Black-and-tan print fabric: ½ yard

- Novelty print fabric: ¼ yard (try something quirky)

- Dark gold center square fabric: 1 strip 2½″ × 40″

- Sashing and binding fabric: ⅝ yard

- Backing fabric: 1⅜ yards

- Muslin for foundations: ⅔ yard

CUTTING

Refer to pages 10–11 for strip cutting and pressing.

From 2 dark red prints:
Cut 20 strips 1½″ wide.

From 2 medium red prints:
Cut 10 strips 1½″ wide.

From 2 muted gold prints:
Cut 15 strips 1½″ wide.

From 3 black prints:
Cut 18 strips 1½″ wide.

From black-and-tan prints:
Cut 10 strips 1½″ wide

From novelty print:
Cut 3 strips 1½″ wide.

From dark gold center square fabric:
Cut 12 squares 2½″ × 2½″.

From sashing and binding fabric:
Cut 4 strips 1½″ wide for sashing, and 4 strips 3″ wide for double-fold or 2″ wide for single-fold binding.

From muslin:
Cut 12 squares 7″ × 7″ for foundations.

Directions

MAKE THE BLOCKS

Refer to pages 14–15 for Traditional Log Cabin block construction, pages 12–13 for Courthouse Steps block construction, and page 14 for Courthouse Steps Squared construction.

1. For each block, position a 2½″ center square on a marked foundation.

2. Construct the blocks as described below.

Strip quantities called out in each block illustration refer to the number of width-of-fabric (WOF) strips needed to complete the block.

1A	1B
2A	2B
3A	3B
4A	4B
5A	5B
6A	6B

Block 1A Courthouse Steps

Rounds 1–10: gold for A and C (novelty print, row 4), black-and-tan print for B and D

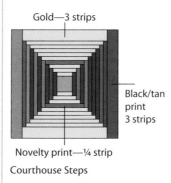

Gold—3 strips

Black/tan print 3 strips

Novelty print—¼ strip

Courthouse Steps

Block 2A Courthouse Steps Squared

Rounds 1–3: dark red

Round 4: gold

Rounds 5–10: black

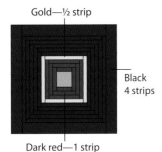

Gold—½ strip

Black 4 strips

Dark red—1 strip

Courthouse Steps Squared

Block 3A Courthouse Steps and Courthouse Steps Squared

Round 1: light red for A and C, dark red for B and D

Rounds 2–8: light red for A and C, black for B and D

Round 10: black

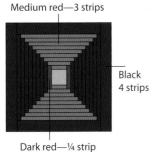

Medium red—3 strips

Black 4 strips

Dark red—¼ strip

Courthouse Steps and Courthouse Steps Squared

Block 4A Courthouse Steps Squared

Rounds 1–6: black

Round 7: gold

Rounds 8–10: dark red

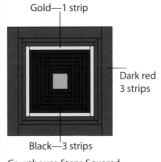

Gold—1 strip

Dark red 3 strips

Black—3 strips

Courthouse Steps Squared

Block 5A Courthouse Steps and Courthouse Steps Squared

Rounds 1–8: dark red for A and C, gold for B and D (1 dark red strip, row 4)

Rounds 9–10: medium red

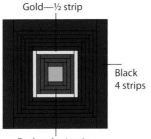

Gold—½ strip

Black 4 strips

Dark red—1 strip

Courthouse Steps and Courthouse Steps Squared

Block 6A Courthouse Steps: Log Cabin Soup

10 Rounds: leftover fabric strips

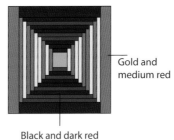

"Leftovers"

Gold and medium red

Black and dark red

Courthouse Steps: Log Cabin Soup

Block 1B Courthouse Steps Squared

Rounds 1–2: black

Round 3: gold

Rounds 4–10: dark red

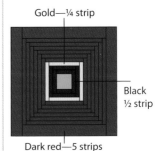

Gold—¼ strip

Black ½ strip

Dark red—5 strips

Courthouse Steps Squared

Block 2B Traditional Log Cabin

Round 1: medium red for A and B, dark red for C and D

Rounds 2–10: alternating medium red and gold for A and B, alternating dark reds for C and D

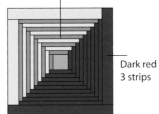

Gold alternating with medium red—1½ strips each

Dark red 3 strips

Traditional Log Cabin

Block 3B Courthouse Steps and Courthouse Steps Squared

Round 1: dark red

Rounds 2–8: black for A and C, black-and-tan print for B and D

Rounds 9–10: dark red

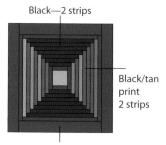

Black—2 strips

Black/tan print 2 strips

Dark red—2 strips

Courthouse Steps and Courthouse Steps Squared

Block 4B Courthouse Steps and Courthouse Steps Squared

Round 1: black

Rounds 2–7: novelty print for A and C, dark red for B and D

Rounds 8–10: gold

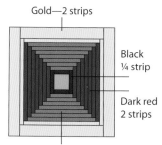

Gold—2 strips

Black ¼ strip

Dark red 2 strips

Novelty print—2 strips

Courthouse Steps and Courthouse Steps Squared

Block 5B Traditional Log Cabin

Rounds 1–10: medium red for A and B (dark red, row 5), black for C and D

Medium red—3 strips

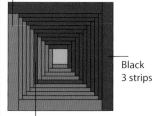

Black 3 strips

Dark red—½ strip

Traditional Log Cabin

Block 6B Courthouse Steps Squared

Rounds 1–10: Alternating gold and black-and-tan print

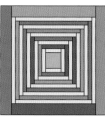

Gold alternating with black/tan print 3 strips each

Courthouse Steps Squared

ASSEMBLY, SASHING, AND FINISHING

Refer to pages 16–18 for block assembly, sashing, and finishing.

1. Square up the blocks, and determine their placement on a design wall. Take some time to move them around. Note the interesting shading that can appear as the blocks interact (see *Autumn Leaves* on page 34).

2. When you are satisfied with your block arrangement on the design wall, zigzag stitch the blocks together, using the widest zigzag stitch on your machine.

3. Sash over the zigzag stitch.

4. Place the quilt on the backing, and pin everything in place.

5. Quilt the sashing in your preferred method.

6. Bind the quilt with single- or double-fold binding. The binding should be approximately ⅜" to ½" wide, to cover the outside edge of the blocks.

GALLERY OF SAMPLER QUILTS

Western Gear, 30″ × 27″, made by Sarah Kaufman, 2007

This quilt features an antique singletree hanger. The painted gourds, found in Vancouver, B.C., inspired the color scheme.

Autumn Leaves, 13½″ × 40½″, made by Stephanie G. Landis, 2008

This table runner has leaf bead embellishments.

Maple Blondie, 14½″ × 21½″, made by Pat Jones, 2009

This is a memory quilt for Pat—maple blondies were a treat from her past.

Fungus Among Us, 37″ × 37″, made by Sarah Kaufman, 2008

I love mushrooms—my fabric stash reflects this passion. As is often the case, no two blocks are identical.

Sixty Cents

Finished block size: 5″ × 5″   **Finished quilt size:** 15″ × 20″

Sixty Cents, made by Sarah Kaufman, 2009

This is my favorite Courthouse Steps design. I call it Love Thy Neighbor, because each quadrant unites and becomes one with its nearest neighboring block. All you need is fabric variety, be it low contrast, opposites on the color wheel, or simply lots of scraps from your stash. The other necessary ingredient is a design wall. You do need to look at and plan your quilt as it expands block by block.

The following instructions for Sixty Cents *can easily be translated into a larger quilt. You might wish to expand and rename this piece* One Dollar *(eight additional nickels in eight more blocks).*

MATERIALS

Fabric note: Why "*Sixty Cents*"? I love the neutrals brown and tan. But they can be both rich **and** boring without some spice. Adding splashes of coral tones, and shiny **nickels** in the center pockets, gives this piece the spark it needed. The 6 darker quadrants at the top and bottom create a border effect, pleasing in a piece where the sashing blends in.

- Medium-value fabrics: ¼ yard each of 16 fabrics for full Neighbor blocks, side half Neighbor blocks, and sashing

- Dark-value fabric: ⅓ yard for top and bottom half Neighbor blocks

- Center square fabric: 1 strip 2″ × 28″

- Binding fabric: ¼ yard

- Backing fabric: ¾ yard

- Muslin for foundations: ½ yard

CUTTING

Refer to pages 10–11 for strip cutting and pressing.

From 16 medium-value fabrics: Cut 3 strips 1½″ wide.

From darker fabric: Cut 5 strips 1½″ wide.

From center square fabric: Cut 12 squares 2″ × 2″.

From each full Neighbor fabric: Cut 1 strip 6¼″ long, to be pieced for sashing.

From muslin: Cut 12 squares 5″ × 5″ for foundations.

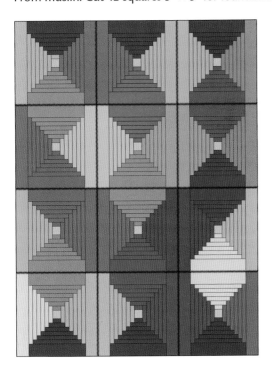

Directions

MAKE THE BLOCKS

Refer to pages 12–13 for Courthouse Steps block construction.

Note: Begin with one of the **2 middle** full Neighbor blocks.

1. Position a 2″ square on a marked foundation.

2. Cut 1 strip 2″ long from each of **4 different** fabrics. Place the first 2 strips at A and C, and stitch at ⅜″. Then stitch the remaining strips at B and D.

First round of strips

Note: Always begin with A and C. B and D are sewn last. The final strips for B and D always finish **longer** than A and C.

3. Stitch the strips, and continue with 6 more rounds of strips to complete the block. With 3 strips 40″ long, you will have ample to use each fabric for 3 quadrants in full Neighbor blocks plus 1 side quadrant.

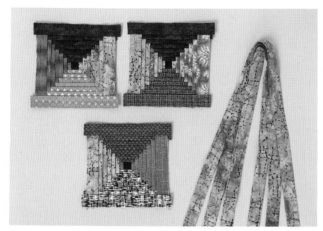

3 strips for 3 quadrants

4. Use your design wall as you work out from the first block in each direction, matching B and D sides and A and C sides. Pay attention as each block is sewn.

Match blocks as you go.

ASSEMBLY, SASHING, AND FINISHING

Refer to pages 16–18 for block assembly, sashing, and finishing.

1. Square up the blocks.

2. Zigzag stitch them together, using the widest zigzag stitch on your machine.

3. My blended version of sashing is nice for using leftover strips. Match up each 6¼″-long strip of feature fabric with coordinating Neighbor blocks (steam press these strips open if they were folded).

4. Begin by covering the 2 vertical seams. Sash using 6¼″-long pieces (rather than full-length strips), and slightly overlap at each intersection. These overlapped areas will be covered by the horizontal sashing.

5. Press the sashing over the zigzagged area, and blind-stitch in place.

6. For the horizontal sashing, measure and trim strips to fit, seam the ends together using a ¼″ seam allowance, and press them open. Place with the seams centered at each intersection, covering the vertical overlapping. Stitch, press, and blindstitch in place.

Vertical sashing with final horizontal sashing ready

7. Place the quilt on the backing, and pin everything in place.

8. Use the Crow Footing stitch (pages 17–18) on the sashing, or quilt with another stitch of your choice.

9. Bind the quilt with single- or double-fold binding. The binding should be approximately ⅜″ to ½″ wide, to cover the outside edge of the blocks.

GALLERY OF COURTHOUSE STEPS VARIATION QUILTS

Look at the Love Thy Neighbor quilts and note how different they appear with **contrasting** sashing. *Birthday Cake* (below) is the same size and uses the same block assembly as *Sixty Cents*, but it looks like a third cousin once-removed.

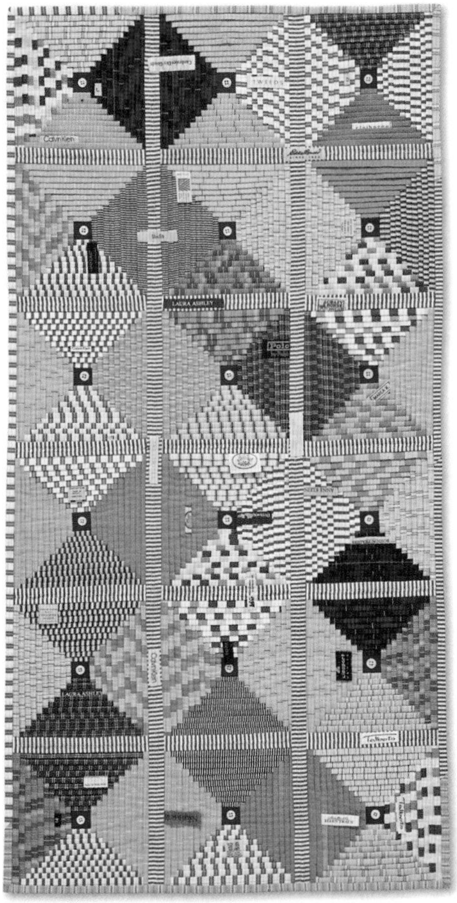

Shirts, 23″ × 45″, made by Sarah Kaufman, 1999

We were moving to Hawaii. Our long-sleeve mainland shirts, including some buttons and labels, were recycled into my first Love Thy Neighbor quilt.

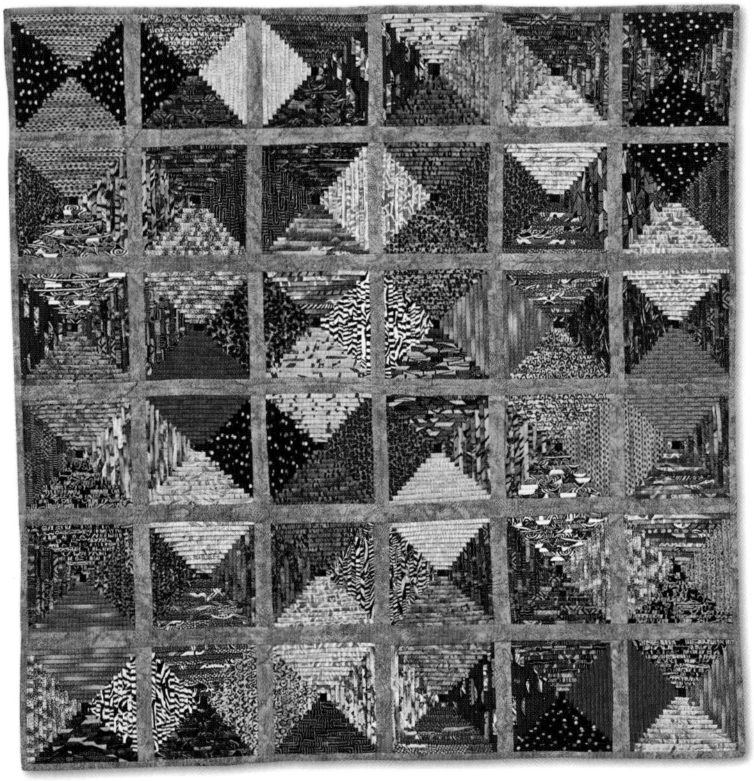

Out of Africa, 41″ × 41″, made by Ardith Younger, 2007

Ardie featured a collection of African prints in her first Folded Log Cabin quilt.

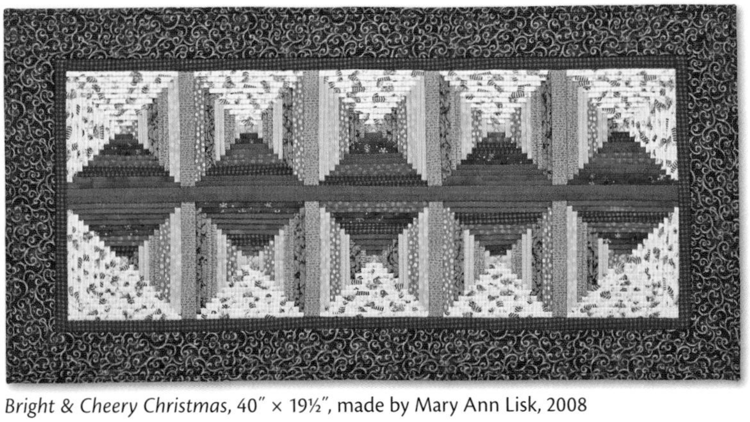

Bright & Cheery Christmas, 40″ × 19½″, made by Mary Ann Lisk, 2008

From the collection of Judy Harbin.

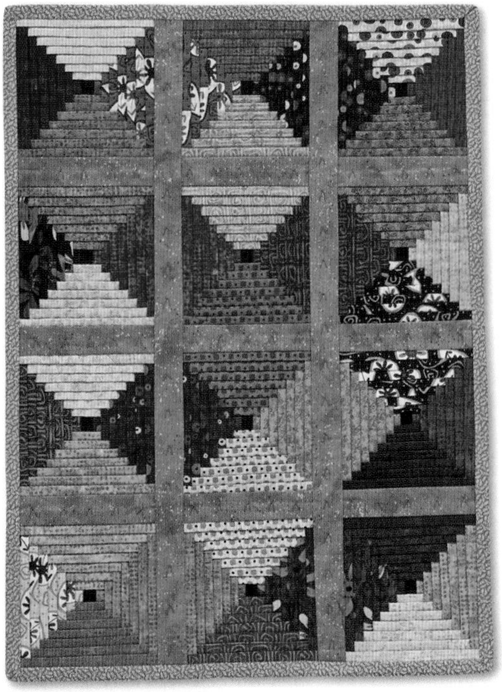

Birthday Cake, 15″ × 20″, made by Sarah Kaufman, 2009

Crayon Houses

Finished block size: 7½″ × 7½″   **Finished quilt size:** 28½″ × 23″

Crayon Houses, made by Sarah Kaufman, 2009

*My first-grade drawings were usually of houses. I am a retired real estate agent, and I am a homebody. I love houses, in real life and in quilts. There is no end to Folded Log **Cabins** in my mental storehouse of home plans.*

As you study this collection of house quilts, you will note that the basic house is made in Courthouse Steps Squared block style. The roof, in each case, is Courthouse Steps, with sky fabric used for three segments and roof fabric for the final segment.

MATERIALS

- 3 house body fabrics: ⅓ yard each

- 3 roof fabrics: ¼ yard each

- Sky fabric: ⅞ yard

- House center square fabric (to contrast with house body fabrics): 2½″ × 10″ strip

- Lane fabric: ⅛ yard

- Green grass fabric: 1½″ × 9″ strip

- Border fabric: 1 yard striped fabric (for 2 cross-grain strips and 2 lengthwise strips) **OR** ½ yard striped fabric (for 4 cross-grain strips)

- Muslin for foundations: ½ yard

- Backing fabric: ¾ yard

- Binding fabric: ½ yard

- Batting for borders: 2 strips 5″ × 21″; 2 strips 5″ × 25″

CUTTING

Refer to pages 10–11 for strip cutting and pressing.

From each of 3 house fabrics: Cut 6 strips 1½″ wide.

From each of 3 roof fabrics: Cut 2 strips 1½″ wide.

> From the first of each roof-strip pair: Cut 1 piece 1½″ × 9″ to reserve for block sashing. Do not fold these subcuts.

From house center square fabric: Cut 2½″ × 2½″ squares for 3 house body centers.

From **either** sky fabric or roof fabric: Cut 2½″ × 2½″ squares for 3 sky and roof centers (see Make the Blocks, Step 3).

From sky fabric: Cut 15 strips 1½″ wide.

> From a sky strip: Cut 2 pieces 1½″ × 14″ to reserve for vertical sashing.

From green grass fabric: Cut 2 pieces 1½″ × 4½″ for vertical sashes to piece with sky sashes.

From lane fabric: Cut 1 strip 3″ × 24″; this will be trimmed to fit houses.

From border fabric: Cut 2 cross-grain side pieces 4″ × 18″ and 2 lengthwise top/bottom pieces 4″ × 32″.

From muslin: Cut 6 squares 7½″ × 7½″ for foundations.

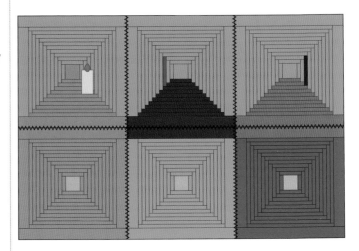

Directions

MAKE THE BLOCKS

Refer to pages 12–13 for Courthouse Steps block construction and page 14 for Courthouse Steps Squared construction.

1. For the body of a house, center a 2½″ square on a marked foundation.

> With my first Crayon House, I was not pleased with the contrast of the center square after the house body block was completed. **I inserted a new 1¼″ square into the pocket.** You can do this to any Folded Log Cabin block.

2. Begin the house body construction (a Courthouse Steps Squared block) by stacking 11 rounds of strips for a 7½″ block. The **final** strip (D)—the top of the house block—can be the roofing fabric.

3. For the sky and roof (a Courthouse Steps block), make a 7½″ block with 11 rounds of strips. For A, C, and B use sky fabric; for D use roof fabric. The 2½″ center square for this block can be from the rooftop or the sky fabric.

4. Repeat Steps 1–3 for 2 more houses.

Note: In my house quilts, I often add chimneys as a contrasting strip in the sky section, or in tag form, tucked into a seam. *Penny Lane* and *Indigo Sky over Mura* (both on page 42) have terra-cotta beads used for chimneys.

ASSEMBLY, SASHING, AND FINISHING

Refer to pages 16–18 for block assembly, sashing, and finishing.

1. Square up the blocks, and determine their placement on a design wall.

2. When you are satisfied with your block arrangement on the design wall, zigzag stitch the blocks together, using the widest zigzag stitch on your machine.

3. For sashing, first sash the 3 horizontal roof-to-house body joints with a 1½″ × 9″ roof fabric strip. These can be overlapped at each intersection (the overlapped area will be covered by the vertical sashing strips). Stitch each strip, press over the zigzagged seam, and hand stitch to the adjoining block.

4. For the final vertical sashing, seam the sky and grass strip ends together with a ¼″ seam allowance, and press them open. You are the landscaper—you determine the positioning of the grass in relation to the sky! Stitch these final vertical sashing strips, press over the zigzag seam, and hand stitch to the adjoining blocks.

5. Measure the width of the houses, and cut the lane fabric to match. Stitch the lane to the bottom of the quilt, and press.

6. For the borders, with the horizontal stripe effect shown, first measure the height of the house blocks with the lane attached, and re-cut the two cross-grain strips to this measurement. Make sure the stripes are perpendicular to the long sides of the strips. Stitch the borders to the sides, and press. Measure the width of the quilt with the side borders on, and re-cut the two lengthwise strips to this measurement. Make sure the stripes are parallel to the long sides of the strips. Stitch the borders to the top and bottom, and press.

7. Add batting strips to the border (refer to page 17 for adding batting to the border).

8. Place the quilt on the backing, and pin everything in place.

9. Quilt the sashing, lane, and border with your preferred method. I used perle cotton.

10. Bind the quilt with single- or double-fold binding.

Home Decorating

My embellishment stash and trips to a bead and jewelry-making store are my primary sources for home décor. Buttons, beads, labels, and jewelry box items can be windows, door handles—you name it. The doors in *Penny Lane* (page 42) are fabric layered with fast2fuse interfacing (see Resources, page 48) and then satin stitched and tacked down; the lane is made from 1½″ Folded Log Cabin blocks (1 round each), with pennies inserted in the centers. In *Indigo Sky over Mura* (page 42), the structure on the right is my version of a place of business in the neighborhood. In Japan, a drape called a *noren* over the door signifies that the store (or café) is open; the trees are from a bead store.

GALLERY OF HOUSE QUILTS

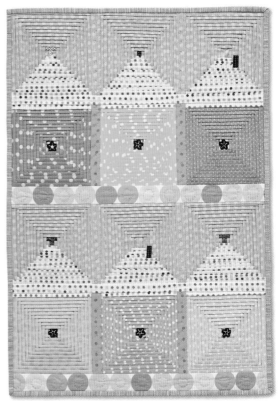

Row Houses, Astoria, 42″ × 21″, made by Sarah Kaufman, 2001

The white house in the middle of the block was my very first home, in Astoria, Oregon, and this quilt was my first Folded Log Cabin Little House. For the border, I used leftover strips—pressed open and pieced in four-patch squares. The density of this border equaled that of the Folded Log Cabin blocks, so no batting was added.

Easter Egg Houses on Polka Dot Street, 25″ × 35″, made by Sarah Kaufman, 2008

It was early March in Bend and still snowing. I yearned for Easter and spring pastels! A trip to the Stitchin' Post in nearby Sisters saved that day! Polka dots always add cheer.

Penny Lane, 23½″ × 17″, made by Sarah Kaufman, 2008

London-like row houses, based on rectangular blocks this time. The windows and doodads for doorknobs came from a bead shop. The lane is highlighted with pennies.

Indigo Sky over Mura (Village), 27½″ × 24″, made by Sarah Kaufman, 2008

In 2004, I traveled to Japan with a group of quilters from Hawaii. The annual Yokohama Quilt Show was our ultimate destination. Along the way we visited some enchanting villages and even toured an indigo dye factory. This was a trip of a lifetime for textile enthusiasts!

Goldie, 24½″ × 31″, made by Sarah Kaufman, 2005

Flat gold discs were used instead of quilting on the sashing. Perle cotton thread was densely stitched on the borders.

Newsprint, 36″ × 45″, made by Sarah Kaufman, 2008

The newsprint-like blocks were inspired by the rolled Vietnamese newsprint coasters sewn to the sashing.

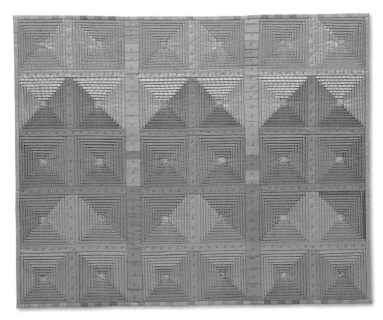

Streak of Lightning, 42″ × 34″, made by Sarah Kaufman, 2008

A wonderful stripe fabric dictated the streak selections. It was used for the binding, plus fussy cut and reassembled for the vertical sashing. Cherished hand-dyed fabric (scraps!) from Kauai became the centers.

Red Rickrack, 39″ × 31″, made by Sarah Kaufman, 2001

Using just red and white would be too lame. Adding busy pink prints gave this piece spice.

Banana Appeal, 47″ × 52″, made by Sarah Kaufman, 2007

A low-contrast quilt honoring my favorite fruit. The bruises that all bananas have can be found in the border fabric.

Fish on a Stick, 21½″ × 29½″, made by Sarah Kaufman, 2008

First came the wooden fish, then George, my stick buddy, came up with the perfect hanger. I shirred the vertical fabric between the blocks to look like a wicker fishing creel.

Liberty Lanterns, 13″ × 29″, made by Sarah Kaufman, 2006

A 3-yard Liberty of London skirt, saved for 20 years, was finally cut up for this piece. I found the old hanger at an outdoor antique fair.

Indigo Dye Works, Kyoto, 19″ × 31″, made by Sarah Kaufman, 2007

The indigo fabrics featured beneath the Courthouse Steps blocks are mostly very old scraps, pulled from a barrel at the indigo dye works in Japan. One piece had even been patched.

Christmas Gents, 22″ × 27″, made by Louise Farm, 2009

Louise included her own needlepoint Santa squares in this seasonal wall quilt.

Off the Beaten Path, 38″ × 46″, made by Sarah Kaufman, 2007

From the collection of Drs. Jim and Ginny Murtaugh. A friend gave me hunks of hand-dyed fabric ravelings. I slit a strip of fabric, wove the strings in, and made tassels to suspend from beads. My working title for this piece was *The Swamp Quilt*.

Spindle and Blocks, 11″ × 50″,
made by Sarah Kaufman, 2007

An antique spindle shows off the fabulous ribbon I found at the Stitchin' Post. A full spectrum of solid fabrics came into play. What fun to make it all work.

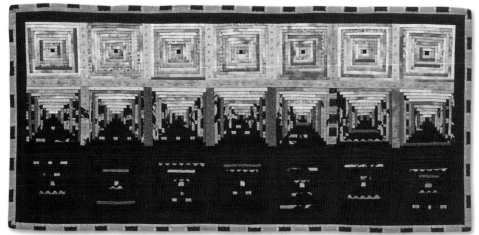

The Penny Loafer Quilt, 47" × 22", made by Sarah Kaufman, 1999

Brown, cordovan, and black—all shoe tones—with pennies inserted. A lovely childhood memory. In addition to the coins, I added wide gold rickrack to the black blocks to liven them up.

Ad Man, 22" × 22", made by Diana Swenson, 2009

Diana used menswear hues to salute her dad, who was a dapper ad man. An embroidery stitch on her machine created the quilting on the sashing.

Fish in the Cabins, 21" × 21", made by Janet Gehlert, 2007

Janet found the collection of Balinese fish blocks in Hawaii. Batik fabrics created the framing in Courthouse Steps Squared style.

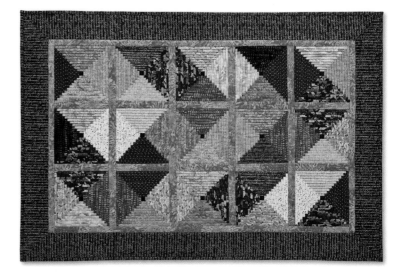

Long Life and Harmony, 41" × 27", made by Mary Ann Lisk, 2007

Mary Ann is a Love Thy Neighbor fan. Many muted floral prints evoke a serene Asian feeling.

About the Author

Sarah Pasma Kaufman and husband, Rich, returned to Oregon in 2005, following home-construction, cultural and sailing adventures in Shaw Island, Washington, and Haleiwa, Hawaii. They may or may not build another house in their future, but two things are for certain: Bend, Oregon, is where they shall remain, and Folded Log Cabin quilts will continue to be Sarah's passion.

Her love of teaching this process has made her a fixture at the Stitchin' Post in nearby Sisters. Just in case you think Folded Log Cabin is Sarah's only thing—six adorable grandchildren all need bed quilts periodically. She continues to take quilt classes of all kinds. Sarah is a member of the Hawaii Quilt Guild in Honolulu, Hawaii, and Mountain Meadow Quilters in Sunriver, Oregon. Her message to quilters everywhere is, "Have a quilt guild in your life." Guilds provide all the inspiration, skill enhancement, friendship, challenge, and opportunity for giving back to your community you could want, and then some!

Resources

Superior Threads
MasterPiece (50-weight),
MasterPiece prewound
bobbins
www.superiorthreads.com

Clover
sashiko needles
www.clover-usa.com

C&T Publishing
fast2fuse double-sided
stiff fusible interfacing
www.ctpub.com

American & Efird, Inc.
Mettler silk-finish cotton
thread (50-weight)
www.amefird.com

The Stitchin' Post
P.O. Box 280
311 Cascade
Sisters, OR 97759
541.549.6061
www.stitchinpost.com

For quilting supplies:

COTTON PATCH MAIL ORDER

3404 Hall Lane, Dept. CTB
Lafayette, CA 94549
800-835-4418; 925-283-7883

Email: CottonPa@aol.com
Website: www.quiltusa.com

Tips and Techniques *can be found at www.ctpub.com >*
Consumer Resources > Quiltmaking Basics: Tips & Techniques for
Quiltmaking & More

For a list of other fine books from C&T Publishing, ask for a free catalog:

C&T PUBLISHING, INC.

P.O. Box 1456
Lafayette, CA 94549
800-284-1114

Email: ctinfo@ctpub.com
Website: www.ctpub.com

C&T Publishing's professional photography services are now available
to the public. Visit us at www.ctmediaservices.com.